Basic Principles of
Violin Playing

by

Paul Rolland

One of a Series of Reports issued by the
MENC String Instruction Committee

Gilbert R. Waller, University of Illinois, Urbana, National Chairman

Originally published byPaul Rolland in 1960.
Copyright ©2000 by Clara Rolland.
All rights reserved.
Printed in the United States of America.
ISBN 1-883026-20-2
No part of this publication may be reproduced by any means whatsoever without the prior writ-
ten permission of the copyright owner.
For information, write Tichenor Publishing, Division of T.I.S., Inc., P.O. Box 669, Bloomington,
Indiana 47402-0669.

Training in **The Rolland Approach to String Teaching** is offered by a number of colleges and universities. For more information please contact:

ASTA with NSOA
1806 Robert Fulton Drive, Suite 300
Reston, VA 20191

Rolland String Research Associates
1616 West Mountain View Drive
Mesa, Arizona 85201
Attn: Dr. Peter Rolland

FOREWORD

Paul Rolland died in 1978 having left a remarkable, *unique* legacy for the string instrument playing/teaching world. His innovative methodology revolutionized string teaching, opening the door to new ideas based on the physical movements essential to playing the violin. Many artists and teachers of note have endorsed his work, including Yehudi Menuhin, Max Rostal, Josef Gingold, Eduard Melkus, Victor Aitay, George Perlman, Paul Doktor, William Primrose, and Roman Totenberg.

Paul Rolland was a founding member of the American String Teachers Association and the first editor of *The American String Teacher*. He is regarded by many as a seminal figure in the scholarship of string pedagogy.

ASTA with NSOA is indebted to Clara Rolland for giving her permission for this reprinting of *Basic Principles of Violin Playing*. We extend our appreciation as well to Boosey & Hawkes, who released publication rights so that ASTA with NSOA might bring this publication to those involved in string instrument playing and teaching. It should by noted that this is a copy of the original text, thus it is an historical document. The changes made are editorial in nature and will, hopefully, be of benefit to the reader.

Mrs. Rolland wishes to express "special recognition of heartfelt thanks to Marla Mutschler who unfailingly and most successfully devoted her energies to the teaching of Paul Rolland's string pedagogy all through the years after his untimely death in 1978"; likewise "thanks to Anne Mischakoff Heiles, who generously contributed much time and effort toward this project."

My sincere gratitude is expressed to the three excellent proofreaders—persons who have had strong interest in Rolland's thought and teachings: Anne Mischakoff Heiles, Kathleen Horvath and Marla Mutschler. Their careful and thoughtful attention to detail is appreciated.

Robert L. Cowden
Publications Chair, ASTA with NSOA

CONTENTS

Section One

TEACHING VIOLIN FUNDAMENTALS

Section Two

INTERMEDIATE—ADVANCED LEVEL

Section One

Teaching Violin Fundamentals

Violin Fundamentals

The student's first goal should be to learn how to produce tone, and for this end his immediate task is to learn how to hold the violin and bow properly. Since it takes time and considerable muscular control to take correct possession of the instrument and bow, the first lesson should be devoted to the exercising of muscular controls so that the necessary skills will develop as rapidly as possible.

The basic formula for technical success is naturalness. The holding and playing movements should be performed in such a fashion that maximum results may be attained with a minimum expenditure of energy. *The correct holding of the instrument and bow should be effected in such a fashion that hands and fingers retain maximum resemblance to their natural resting position.* For instance, the fingers of the right hand are practically in a perfect position for holding the bow when the arm is hanging down at the side. In this position a pencil can be slipped in the pupil's hand, at once giving him the correct feel for holding the bow. A similarly relaxed attitude should be desired in the neck and shoulder area. Permanent raising of the shoulder, or constant twisting of the head to the left, create unrelieved muscular tension in the areas involved, a condition neither healthy nor wise. Any one part of the body that is held in a static position for a considerable length of time will stiffen and thus create a technical hazard as well as a conscious or subconscious discomfort. The easy way of playing the violin is the natural way, in which all parts of the body, changing their relative positions almost continually, are ideally in a fluid motion, never allowing a muscular lock in any part of the body.

Holding the Bow

It is easy to establish a natural way of holding the bow. The student should observe and get the feel of the hand when hanging relaxed at his side. When holding the bow, the hand should have a similarly relaxed feeling and shape. As a first step, pick up the bow with the left hand below the middle, hold it in front, well away from the body; then bring the relaxed hand over the frog. The middle finger and thumb, in opposing one another, serve as a fulcrum to the grip. The upper right corner of the thumbnail member supports the stick just in front of the end-bump of the frog; the middle finger—preferably with its first crease—supports the opposite side of the stick.

The thumb–middle finger–bow junction is the axis around which positive and negative forces act upon the bow. The little finger in a naturally rounded position rests with its tip on the top-back of the stick, and the ball of the ring finger rests on the side of the frog or stick (or both) pulling it gently back toward the palm. The thumb, second, third, and fourth fingers are in charge of supporting the bow, while the first finger rather passively rests on the top of the bow, and has the role of transmitting pressure from the relaxed arm into the string as well as making more delicate shadings on its own. The fingers should not be closed too tightly, nor should they be spread apart too far; rather, they should resemble the natural resting position of the hand.

Applying Pressure (Positive Pressure)
When approaching the tip
Crescendo
Forte
Accents

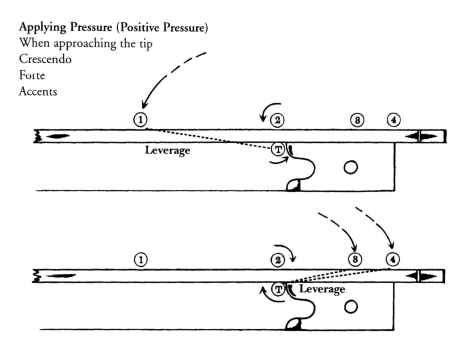

Supporting the Bow (Negative Pressure)
When approaching the frog
Diminuendo
Piano
Lifting bow

The front part of the grip (the thumb–middle finger axis and the first finger) is the agent for applying pressure upon the bow (when approaching the tip, in crescendo, forte playing, accents). The back part of the grip (the thumb–middle finger axis, and the ring and little fingers) is the agent for supporting the bow when approaching the frog, in diminuendo, soft playing, lifting the bow.

In a well-balanced bow grip, the leverages created by the front part of the grip (T-1) and the back part of the grip (T-3, T-4) are sufficiently large, keeping enough distance between thumb–first finger on one side and between thumb–little finger on the other. Therefore it is advisable to adhere strictly to the thumb–middle finger axis, and not to slip the fingers upward on the bow, allowing the ring or even the little finger to oppose the thumb. This latter deviation in holding the bow facilitates playing near the tip, but usually gives poor results at the frog (poor tone control, poor lifted strokes, and clumsiness at the frog).

Silent Bow Exercises

The skill of the hand and fingers in balancing the bow can be greatly promoted by the use of a few simple silent exercises. These are especially helpful in class teaching, where it is advisable to keep students constantly occupied (for more than one reason). These silent gymnastics can be practiced by the class while the teacher works with an individual student.

The "Teeter-Totter"

For developing the balancing skill of the little and ring fingers:

Bow held in horizontal position in front of the player and the little and ring fingers alternately pull or push the bow while the thumb and middle finger serve as an axis. During the "pull," the fingers are well curved, with the hand knuckles of the third and fourth fingers flat. At the end of the "push" the fingers are more relaxed, straighter, and the hand knuckles more prominent. The "teeter-totter" helps bow balancing.

"Press-Release"

For increasing the strength of the thumb and first finger and for tone control:

Bow held in a relaxed and correct fashion, left hand helps to support the bow at the tip. On "press" roll arm inward (elbow slightly rises), lean with the first finger against the stick, with thumb supporting pressure from below (positive pressure); two-three-four, hold pressure, keeping stick and hair pressed together. On "release," take pressure off the first finger by rolling the arm outward (elbow slightly lowers) and support bow with thumb, second, ring, and little fingers (negative pressure); two-three-four, hold hand in rounded relaxed position. On "press" do not merely press the first finger with its own power, but keep it rather passive, leaning against the top of the bow with it, transmitting pressure due to the inward rolling of the arm by the pull of the index finger, the main knuckle of which is approximately level with the stick. On "release" the first finger knuckle rises, and the index finger merely touches the far side of the bow.

Holding the Violin

Principle of Support

The violin should be placed in a position that permits a comfortable reach of the bow when playing either at the tip or frog, with the hair forming a right angle with the string. The left hand also should be accommodated by placing the violin at an angle with the shoulder line that permits reaching the highest positions without undue strain.

For the average person, the button can be placed directly in front of the center of the neck, resting the instrument on the right bump of the left collar bone. The weight of the head is released into the chinrest through the side of the chin, to effect a hold. The violin scroll then should be placed so as to permit reaching the bow tip without strain. The tilt of the violin can be set by keeping the bow slightly below the horizontal when placed on both the G and D strings at once. The elbow should be kept clear of the chest, high enough to hold the violin slightly above horizontal.

The instrument is balanced on the collarbone and the left thumb, which offers its support at the lowest point of the neck when on the G string, and somewhat to

4

the left of this point when on the higher strings. The instrument is further stead-
ied by the chin and by a gentle contact at the base of the first finger. The contact
with the thumb is effected slightly above or below the inner crease of the nail-joint
of the thumb, depending upon the length of the thumb and also upon the string
employed. A lower contact for G string playing is generally desirable.

The violin is not locked in between the shoulder and chin, but rather, the left
shoulder and upper arm are kept in as relaxed a manner as possible, prohibiting the
left arm from freezing in one position. Not only the shoulder area, but also the
whole body, should be kept in a natural, unlocked manner, permitting small compensating motions resulting from large and bold movements of the arms, just like
the motions used in throwing a stone or swinging a bat. Thus the small natural
movements of the violin resulting from a relaxed body attitude are not restricted,
especially when sudden irregular bow movements are employed.

The instrument, resting on the collarbone and left thumb (and very gently
against the first finger base in rapid playing), is not locked into a permanent position by the shoulder and chin. Hence the instrument is supported like a bridge (at
least most of the time), and not like a diving board. This free manner of holding
the instrument was recommended by Leopold Auer and is practiced and professed
by players such as Kreisler, Milstein, Primrose, Ricci, Fuchs, Mischakoff, and to a
certain extent by Heifetz, Francescatti, and Spivakowsky, all celebrated for their
phenomenal tone. The quality of tone is greatly enhanced by the active support
received from a live left arm and hand, which are not merely tools of intonation
but lend energy toward maintaining a balanced contact between violin and bow.

The holding of the violin without the aid of the left hand is not encouraged,
and since the instrument is balanced, rather than held tightly, the use of a pad
becomes unnecessary in most cases. The chinrest, however, should be high enough
for a long-necked person, and it should have a well-shaped ridge to keep the instrument in place during descending shifts.

Establishing a Natural Hold of the Violin

Hold the instrument in guitar fashion and place the *left* hand on the rib at
the *right* side of the neck in the third-fourth position, permitting the inside of
the wrist to touch the rib of the violin. Lift the violin with the right hand, placing it on the collarbone so that the button is in front of the center of the neck.
Keep the left hand completely on the right side of the neck, thumb supporting
the lowest point of the neck, fingers rounded above the strings. The first finger
is well-rounded; its base is on the right side of the neck, not underneath it.

Tilt the violin moderately to the right and keep the scroll as much to the front
as feasible without causing undue strain, and high enough to bring strings to a horizontal position. With the left hand on the right side of the neck, the thumb support will be sufficiently under the neck to offer solid opposition to the finger pressure, and the elbow will assume its proper position. To secure the violin from
above, release the relaxed weight of the head through the left side of the chin into
the chinrest. Do not apply a vise-like grip, tightening the shoulder area, and causing skin irritation.

Chinrest

Since Spohr's invention of the chinrest, it has become a generally accepted accessory of the violin. It helps to support the violin, it frees the vibrations of the plate (dampened by contact with the jaw in early times), and it protects the instrument.

Selection of a proper chinrest that complies with the physique of the individual is of paramount importance for the establishment of a natural hold of the violin. In selecting a chinrest, the height, width, and shape should be considered. The longer the neck of the individual, the higher the chinrest he should use. With a chinrest of the proper height, the head will neither slope down inordinately, nor will it have a jacked-up appearance. A player with a large jaw will usually prefer a broad, flat model chinrest, but normally a well-molded ridge on the back of the rest is advisable, as well as a surface which slopes downward toward the top of the violin. These latter factors allow the concentration of support near the neck, thus improving the leverage of the downward force against the fulcrum at the collarbone.

Shoulder Pad

With a well-selected chinrest and well-balanced left arm, the use of a shoulder pad is not a necessity. Those who find it impossible to play without the use of a pad should keep in mind that the instrument should not be locked in with a strongly fixed grip, thus canceling the upward support of the left arm. Indeed, the greatest tension of the shoulder area may be witnessed among those players who hold the instrument rigidly and "hang up" their left arm with fingers clinging to the fingerboard. The disadvantageous leverage of the downward-pulling finger pressure (which goes unopposed by the thumb) places a great burden upon the supporting area and should be avoided, by all means. If the use of a pad is a must for added security and comfort, it should be laid on the shoulder, but must not be compressed with a strong grip of the neck muscles. The relaxed weight of the head is sufficient to effect a secure hold, paired with a gentle support of the left arm and thumb.

Posture

A healthy, upright, yet not stiff posture should be maintained during playing. The weight of the violin and the forward position of the arms should not cause a low, stooping position. The instrument and the arms should be supported not only with the shoulder muscles but also by the back and, to some extent, the diaphragm as well. To get the "feel" of this support, swing both arms up and down with completely relaxed shoulders, propelling the arms with slight impulses coming from the waist. Swing hands as high up as the head, then suddenly stop arms at the peak of the motion and feel the erect, slightly backward slanting position of the torso. This position is best for playing, whether standing or sitting. The weight of the body should be supported without stiffening the knees. A gentle transfer of weight from one foot to the other should take place when broad bowing motions are executed.

When sitting, the body weight should be supported by the legs as well as the seat. Avoid placing both legs forward; the player should sit so that he can jump up from sitting to standing position without shifting his weight.

Silent Left Hand Exercises

The question could be raised: why play silent exercises when it is more interesting to play with the bow? The fact is that in a class situation, silent exercises are of great help, as the class can engage in these while the instructor gives individual attention to any one member of the class. These activities not only help the students' technique, but also save the teacher a great deal of disciplinary trouble.

Shoulder flex. Stand or sit erect, grab right shoulder with left hand. Keep left shoulder relaxed and low and bounce left elbow up and down with a rolling motion of the upper arm. When tired, drop arm and relax.

Palm-up. Proceed as before, then swing hand out in front, in level with the forehead, maintaining the position of the elbow near the center of the chest. Hold until tired, then drop arm, shake hand.

Silent shifting. Establish violin position as before, then shift back and forth between first and fifth positions. Fingers off the string, relaxed and rounded; support the neck by the thumb in the area of the first joint from the tip and by the second phalanx from the tip. The base of the first finger will glide along the right side of the fingerboard, touching it gently, thus adding stability. Keep wrist straight and shuttle back and forth until tired, then drop hand and relax.

Thumb flex. Press fingers on string, then move thumb back and forth (horizontally) as far as it will go until tired, then relax. Move thumb up and down (vertically) until tired, then relax. Move thumb in circular motion until tired, then relax.

Lift-drop. Keep all four fingers on the string, then lift and drop back four times, each finger in turn. Swing fingers far back but do not straighten. The teacher may call out "lift—drop—rest" at a natural reciting speed.

Straight Bowing

Place the bow at the balance point and check for correct hold. Keep fingers naturally rounded; lift and replace fingers that stiffen. Draw a few inches of bow first, then gradually increase length of bow used. Practice patterns on the D string first, then on the others as well.

It is a typical fault to draw the bow in a clockwise curve. To counteract this tendency strive to draw the bow in an opposite arch, i.e., push the bow well forward at the end of down-bows, forearm well-turned inward. At the conclusion of up-bows, pull frog in the opposite direction, back toward the player's chest, wrist slightly arched. As a result of this, the bow should be drawn straight, i.e., the hair at right angles to the string at all times.

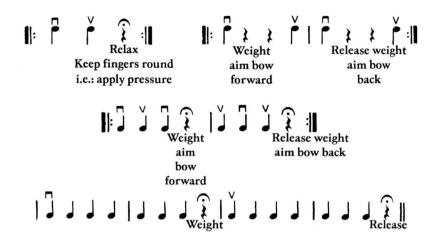

It is a typical fault to draw the bow in a curve opposite to the bow-stick curve:

Typical Fault   **Correction**

Bow Balance

For an even tone, bow pressure and speed must be kept constant at any given contact point of bow and string. Since the bow weight is heavy at the frog and is very light at the tip, the applied bow pressure is constantly changing with the movement of the bow. In approaching the tip, the applied pressure gradually increases, and in approaching the frog the applied pressure gradually decreases. The rate of change is much higher at the lower third of the bow than in the upper two-thirds, this being one of the reasons for greater difficulties when playing at the frog.

To develop good tone production, the student should be encouraged to play with a full tone in the upper part of the bow (positive pressure), and to support the bow well when playing near the frog (negative pressure). In practicing the above bowing patterns, turn the forearm toward the strings, causing the first finger to press the stick when approaching the tip, then hold the stick down during the rest (positive pressure). Then reverse the stroke; beginning with an up-bow, shift the balance toward ring and little fingers, and release pressure from first finger; forearm turned slightly outward, ring finger gently pulling the bow toward the palm, little finger rounded (negative pressure).

Description of Whole-Bow Stroke

A coordinated whole-bow stroke in legato style might be described as follows:*

Down-bow. At the frog the stroke is anticipated with the slightest raise of the elbow; simultaneously, the player inhales.**This preparation eliminates the inertia of the dead-stopped arm, and also gives a feeling of security to the player. As the elbow turns down, the hair is set upon the string with the stick inclining toward the fingerboard; the upper arm (as if turning down from an imaginary up-bow) begins its motion down, away from the body, and slightly back, while the wrist and fingers delay the actual start of the bow with a slight "give." Finally, the bow starts very smoothly, the forearm unfolds, and (very gradually) turns inward, bringing more hair in contact with the string. As the tip approaches, the upper arm reaches forward and also turns, raising the elbow slightly. The hair is now completely flat with the stick directly over it (the latter might even incline slightly toward the bridge). The first finger is directly on top of the stick, transmitting a pulled pressure—that tends to flatten the hand knuckle—due to the inward turning of the arm.

Change of bow at the tip. The change of direction does not occur at the same time in all parts of the arm and bow. Rather, it is a chain procedure, starting in the upper arm, which describes a slight loop (as can be seen in the elbow) either in clockwise or counterclockwise direction. While the arm begins its passage upward, the hand and fingers conclude the down-stroke with a downward motion, and follow the arm through a similar loop into the:

Up-bow stroke. The elbow with the upper arm reverses its movement relaxing the forward reach, and the elbow moves back slightly; the stick turns a little and inclines slightly toward the fingerboard. The forearm then approaches the upper arm, which begins to move up and finally forward. During the up-bow the wrist is slightly higher than during the down-bow, the fingers are a little straighter, and at a sharper angle to the stick. The correct proportion of the movements described above will assure that the bow is drawn parallel with the bridge, or more precisely, at a right angle with the strings.

Change at the frog. At the end of the up-stroke the elbow reaches its peak, then drops slightly before the conclusion of the up-stroke, which is completed with a flexible "follow-through" of the hand and fingers. In approaching the frog, the stick again inclines toward the fingerboard with less hair contacting the string at the very conclusion of the up-bow stroke. The first finger ceases to press the top of the bow and is slightly raised from the top of the stick, but maintains contact on its far side. As the bow is turned down again, the stick turns slightly toward the player, bringing a little more hair (but not all of it) into contact with the string at the beginning of the down-bow.

---

*A "professional" stroke is described here. It takes time to develop a finished, coordinated, stroke.

**This gives confidence in starting a piece or entering after a rest.

9

Tone Quality, Contact Point, Even Division*

Strive for a solid, clear tone quality. Keep the contact point between string and hair steady. If the bow is not drawn straight, the contact point will constantly shift. Develop an alert listening attitude and a high ideal of good tone. Divide the bow evenly; don't start the bow too quickly. In half notes, the second count should fall on the middle; in whole notes, the third count should fall on the middle.

Use a few inches of bow first, soon increase speed and length of bow used. If the bow travels fast, the contact point is somewhat nearer to the fingerboard, and when the bow moves slowly it should be drawn nearer to the bridge. If the tone is thin and whistling, if it is scratchy, choked, the speed and pressure are not matched. Perhaps the movement of the bow is too slow or too fast for the amount of pressure given, or the pressure is too great or too little for the speed. As a rule, strive for a solid and big tone in the upper part of the bow, and avoid excessive pressure near the frog.

String Level, String Crossing

In addition to the to-and-fro movements of the forearm from the elbow, and the small back-and-forth movements of the upper arm from the shoulder, there is one more "large movement" (in the bow arm) to be learned, namely, the vertical movement of the upper arm used in string crossing. This movement can be best observed by the movement and position of the elbow, which should be considerably higher when the bow is on the G string than when playing on the E string. The vertical motion of the upper arm should be executed in a smooth, round fashion, not with a jerky motion. For this, a relaxed shoulder is necessary.

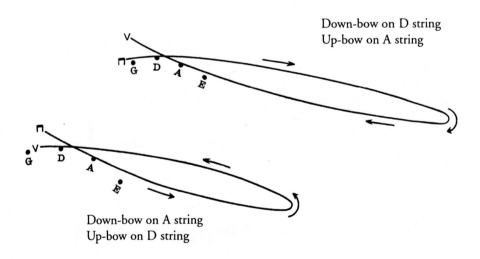

Down-bow on D string
Up-bow on A string

Down-bow on A string
Up-bow on D string

*This topic is further discussed in Section Two.

Place the middle of the bow on the strings and rock the bow silently, with a vertical motion of the upper arm, up and down between G and E strings, and without moving the bow horizontally. The bow and arm form the bow-plane which governs the relation of the upper and lower part of the arm and bow. The bow-plane is higher on the G string and is gradually lower on each of the higher strings.

During string crossings, the vertical motion should take effect slightly before the completion of the horizontal stroke on the string of the first note. The result will be a round, slightly curved movement instead of a jerky one. (See illustration on bottom of page 10.)

Size of Crossing

In fast playing, the size of the crossing should be limited to a minimum. Excess motion is a waste of time and energy. In leisurely speed, it is permissible to enlarge the size of the crossing for a free flowing motion. The vertical motion is considerably larger at the tip than in the vicinity of the frog.*

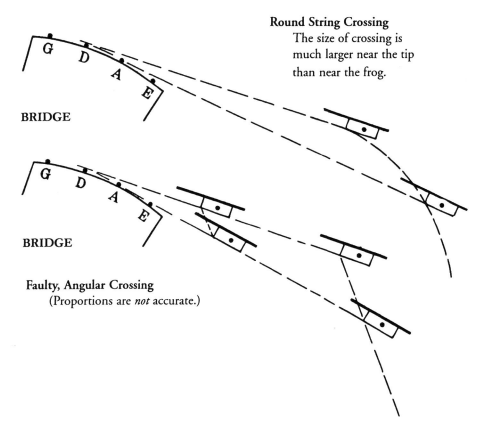

Round String Crossing
The size of crossing is much larger near the tip than near the frog.

BRIDGE

BRIDGE

Faulty, Angular Crossing
(Proportions are *not* accurate.)

*Discussion of bowing continued on page 14 and in Section Two, "Intermediate — Advanced Level" on page 26 and subsequent pages.

Position of Left Hand, Fingers, and Thumb

In discussing this subject, the following terminology will be employed: "elevation," "angle," and "balance." These concepts will aid in describing the possible variations in the position of left hand, fingers, and thumb.

Elevation refers to the height of the hand, the relative position of the hand knuckles to the fingerboard. When the large knuckle of the first finger is in line with the edge of the fingerboard (when playing on the E string) or even higher, we have a relatively high hand position; with the inner crease of the first finger base joint in the same position, the hand is at a median height; if below that, the hand is in a relatively low position. When the neck is permitted to slip into the soft flesh of the thumb, the hand is in too high a position.

Both the high and low positions have certain advantages. When the hand is relatively high, the fingers are better curved, more articulate, due to the more vertical fall of the fingertips. However, in this high position the reach of the fingers, their extension range, is more limited. In the relatively low position the extension range of the fingers is favored, but the finger contact is flatter, impairing the crispness of articulation.

A logical compromise is to place the hand knuckles as high as practicable but not so high that the reach of the fingers thereby becomes restricted.

The *angle* of the fingers is determined by the position of the elbow (in some cases by the ordinary bending of the wrist) under the violin to the left or right.

If the elbow is too far to the left, the fingers interfere with the string on the right side; if it is too far to the right the fingers will not completely stop the string, but will leave it partially uncovered. In a certain placement of the elbow, the fingers will work at peak efficiency in their *best angle*.

The best angle is different for the various strings, the difference between G and E strings being considerable. In melodic playing the best angle should be cultivated for maximum tonal results. The adjustment is made with a rolling hammock-like motion of the upper arm from the shoulder joint, similar to the vertical movement of the right upper arm in string crossing. However, in rapid playing, the maintenance of the best angle is not always possible due to intricate string crossings or simultaneous occupancy of two or more strings. Therefore in rapid playing, an average angle best suited for D and A string playing is often practical, thus minimizing the movements of the arm.

Balance deals with the general accessibility of all four fingers at any time.

The hand is well balanced if all four fingers can reach their respective notes without undue strain. The balance is mainly governed by the position of the wrist and thumb. If the wrist is arched away from the player, the first and second fingers are favored. When the wrist is too hollow and bent toward the player, the third and especially the fourth fingers are favored, but the first and second fingers must be pulled far back and will tend to cramp under the neck. In most cases, the best balance can be established by keeping the wrist in a straight line with the forearm, balancing the hand around the second and third fingers. This, however, is not always possible if the fingers are disproportioned, or if the arm is unusually short.

An ideally balanced hand will have the knuckles nearly parallel with the strings, both in a horizontal and in a vertical plane, allowing an ideally quiet hand in passage and scale work. Unfortunately, this cannot be achieved by all, and allowances must be made due to the physical limitations of certain hands, by permitting a change in the balance of the hand when going to the fourth finger. If the fourth finger cannot reach its note in comfort, a small, almost unnoticeable compensating movement forwarding the wrist and thumb should be permitted. These tiny horizontal movements will be possible only if the thumb and the base of the first finger are flexible and if no horizontal grip exists between thumb and first finger.

The *thumb* should be especially flexible during shifts, where it is important that the thumb break the friction in advance and lean into the direction of the shift. The thumb should constantly seek for the best possible foothold in opposing the pressure of the fingers, and to a certain extent the weight of the violin; its position is ever changing, depending upon the string, position, and—in cantilena playing—even the finger employed.

It is advantageous to offer the thumb support with its main member, since this joint is stronger than the nail phalanx. This high position of the thumb is suitable for many, but if the thumb is short and the hand is broad, it is better to support the neck with the nail phalanx. Similarly, for very large hands, a lower thumb position is often advantageous in order to get the fingers out of the way, and avoid crowding them.

For the balance of the left hand, it is also necessary to turn the left forearm clockwise (supination) and to poise the little finger ahead toward the strings. This attitude is developed by the meticulous observation of keeping the first and fourth fingers down during string crossing, and also by the industrious playing of octaves and thirds. Hence, the sooner these are introduced, the better.

Summary

When the hand is properly *elevated,* the fingers have maximum power; when well *balanced,* the fingerboard becomes accessible to all fingers; and with the best possible *angle,* maximum tonal results can be obtained.

Finger Motion

Silent Percussion

Considerable strength can he gained by silent percussion studies. It is also well known that in a class, rapid finger action when sounded at an early stage usually results in chaos since the coordination and intonation are yet on a very low level.

Write numbers on the board, and have students hold the violin in guitar fashion. Place four fingers on the string correctly in the "2-3" pattern. Lift the violin to correct position, then wiggle the thumb and hand a little to avoid any set, stiff position. Raise the fingers a tiny bit and proceed, tapping fingers in a strict rhythmic fashion according to the following chart or similar ones invented by the teacher or class. Drop fingers swiftly and firmly from the main knuckles and raise them in a quick, electric spark-like fashion.

Play four times (4x) on any string and eventually in all finger patterns.

(1) 0	1	0	1	*(4x)*	(2) 0	1	2	1	*(4x)*	(3) 0	2	1	2	*(4x)*
2	1	2	1	"	1	2	3	2	"	1	3	2	3	"
2	3	2	3	"	2	3	4	3	"	0	2	1	2	"
4	3	4	3	"			Read down, then up.							

Silent Percussion with String Crossing: Play upper numbers on the next highest string, keep fingers down on lower string.

(1) 0 1 2 3 | 0 1 0 1 | 0 1 0 1 | 0 | 3 2 1 | *(Play four times)*

(2) 0 1 2 | 0 1 0 | 2 1 | *(4x)*

(3) 1 2 3 | 0 | 1 0 | 3 | 2 | *(4x)*

(4) 0 1 2 3 | 1 4 | 1 4 | 1 4 | 1 4 | 4 3 2 | *(4x)*

General Suggestions: Begin on G, D, or A string; keep fingers down when possible; meticulously observe this rule where numbers are underlined. Swing finger back from the hand knuckle as far as possible, not upward. Drop fingers, keep thumb and hand flexible.

Other Bowing Patterns

After bowings on page 8 are well under way in the upper and lower half of the bow, learn to draw the whole bow on the open strings or in combination with the fingers.

General suggestions: Keep hair at right angle to the string. Draw bow at even speed, about halfway between bridge and fingerboard with a steady contact point.

At tip: Keep first finger firmly on the bow (positive pressure).

At frog: Release first finger pressure and take hold with rounded third and fourth finger (negative pressure).

(1) 𝄆 ⌐ | ⌐ | ⌐ | - | ⌐ | ⌐ | ⌐ | - 𝄇

Weight
Aim bow forward Bow always straight

Release weight
Aim bow back

(2) 𝄆 ⌐ | ⌐ | ⌐ | ⌐ 𝄇
WB

Even division, straight bowing; count 2 at the middle.

(3) 𝄆 ⌐ | ⌐ ⌐ | ⌐ | ⌐ ⌐ 𝄇
WB   UH   WB   LH

(4) 𝄆 ⌐ ⌐ ♪♪♪♪ 𝄇   For free bowing with swinging forearm strokes.
UH   M

(5) 𝄆 ⌐ ⌐ ⌐ ⌐ | ♪♪♪♪ ♪♪♪♪ 𝄇   For free bowing with swinging forearm strokes.
UH   M

(6) 𝄆 ⌐ ⌐ ⌐ 𝄇   With firm contact after down-bow; release after up-bow.
WB

(7) 𝄆 ⌐ ♪♪♪♪ | ⌐ ♪♪♪♪ 𝄇   Play eighth notes firmly at the tip, with good support and flexibility at the frog.
WB T   WB F

(8) 𝄆 ○ | ○ 𝄇   For even division of the bow. Play with a full tone near the bridge. Use whole bow, count 3 exactly at the middle. Keep bow straight.
WB

Finger Patterns

The spatial sense as well as bowing can be developed with the simple exercises that follow. Notes are first repeated (4x, 3x, 2x) to make intonation easier.

2-3 Pattern	1-2 Pattern	3-4 Pattern	Whole Tone Pattern
0 1 23 4	0 12 3 4	0 1 2 34	0 1 2 3 4

Joined numbers indicate half steps, others whole.

Play with bow and fingers note groups on any string in the four finger patterns. Play each note:

(a) 4x (b) 3x (c) twice (d) once (e) slur 2 (f) slur 4 (g) slur 4

(1) ‖:0 1 3 2:‖ (2) ‖:1 4 3 4:‖ (3) ‖:2 4 3 1:‖

Invent your own. Repeat each group many times.

More Advanced Bowing

The Finger Accent (Piqué)

To develop the bite needed for accentuation and for the staccato and martelé type strokes, the flexibility and skill of the fingers should be developed. This flexibility will also help to make a smooth change of bow possible.

Place the bow on the string with a firm contact at the balance point; the bow is supported by the curved fingers (negative pressure). Suddenly move the bow about an inch by straightening the fingers. Aim for a crystal clear attack and a very short sound free from unpleasant scratches or noises. Release bow pressure immediately upon attack, then rest, and contact string for the next up-bow stroke during which the fingers will suddenly curve again. This stroke is called in French "piqué" ("spurred").

The Martelé and Staccato

Combine the "piqué" with a quick movement of the forearm from the elbow, above the middle. Use quick, short strokes, stopping suddenly after each stroke.

Preparation for Dotted Rhythms

The following rhythms are helpful for the development of coordination between the two hands, and for developing a precise instantaneous change of the bow. *Preparation:*

At the frog and tip with short quick strokes:

(a) Practice near the tip with the bowings marked.
(b) Practice near frog with reversed bowing. At first repeat notes within the rhythmic groups on open strings, and in scales. Later play each note only once in scales and exercises.*

First Shifting

The introduction of early shifting patterns by rote has a good effect on the freedom of the left hand. By early shifting the so-frequent lock between thumb, neck, and first finger can be eliminated. In shifting, the balance of the hand must not be lost. The relative position of fingers, wrist, and fingerboard level should be maintained between the first and fourth position.

Silent Shifting

(a) Place all four fingers lightly without pressure on the string. Support instrument with the right hand or support the scroll against the wall. Shuttle back and forth between first and third or fourth positions; keep position of hand and fingers the same.
(b) Shift with a single finger, and with slight pressure on the string, but keep other fingers poised as if playing with all of them.
(c) Proceed as in (b) but without supporting the instrument with the right hand or wall. Help descending shifts by moving the thumb down in advance of the hand. Practice the lateral movement of the thumb separately also. (Refer to "Thumb Flex," p. 7.)

Shifting, Bow and Fingers

Shift from first to third position, each finger on each string: (a) with detached notes; (b) connected; (c) slurred.

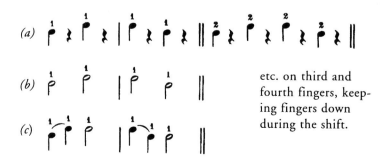

etc. on third and fourth fingers, keeping fingers down during the shift.

* Discussion of bowing continued on pages following and in Section Two.

Play major and minor triads with one finger on one string.

Practice also with the second, third, and fourth fingers.

Minimize the friction between the thumb and the neck before the shift. The preparation of the thumb is more pronounced in the downward shift, and should be aided by leaning with the wrist in the direction of the shift.*

Tone Quality—Intonation

The student's immediate goal should be to learn to produce tone through the basic forms and motions discussed previously. One must keep in mind that the synthesis of the numerous motions and forms used in playing will not alone produce a good and beautiful tone automatically. *A vigilant attitude on the part of the student, constantly selecting the good, rejecting the bad in sound, is of the greatest importance.* The inner concept of a good sound paired with such a critical attitude, plus all other considerations as discussed previously, will lead to success, to the production of a good tone.

Similarly, good intonation can be developed only if the student, absorbed in the sound he is producing, rejects the false and strives for the true. No amount of manual know-how alone will produce a good sound and a good pitch; the manual and physical factors must be paired with audio control. Therefore, the good teacher will constantly urge the student to listen, to appraise, and to correct.

It is impossible to set the hand and fingers in any position that would automatically result in good intonation. Correct intonation is a habit acquired only by attentive practicing and an inherently good ear.

At times the hand and fingers must make strenuous efforts and adjustments to play in tune, and the avoidance of such strains or adjustments results in bad intonation. String players commonly get into habits of faulty intonation because of negligence in making certain extensions, contractions, and hand adjustments when playing certain notes in certain keys. For instance, in the sharped keys, intonation is relatively easy, as the "2-3 pattern" (probably the least strenuous one) is used much of the time. And yet, even in this relatively easy pattern it is very common to play the half steps too wide because it is more comfortable to do so. In the "1-2 pattern" (G major: A string, E string; C major: D string, A string) one has to battle against a too high second finger, and against a much too low fourth finger. The tendency is to play the major third too narrow and the

*Discussion of shifting continued on pages 24-26.

minor third too wide, because it is easier to do so. Likewise, in the flat keys (F major, B♭ major: A and E strings) the first finger does not like to stretch back far enough to the nut but prefers to play sharp; or if finally it is low enough, the third finger often suffers by being too low. The conscientious teacher is aware of these and similar pitfalls and warns the students to avoid them.

Flexibility of the thumb and of the base of the first finger is imperative for good intonation. Small adjustments in the position of the thumb and in the base joint of the first finger must be constantly made to permit a wider reach.

Intonation can be greatly improved by rote playing of scales and sequences. First, study the five-tone major and minor patterns beginning on the open string. Then include the sixth tone for the purpose of learning a smooth string crossing. Finally play the entire scale up and down. After learning the G, D, A majors beginning with the open string, play the minor scales starting on the open strings. Then follow up with the major scale beginning on the first finger A, E, B♭, E♭ majors. With the pattern of the A major scale, beginning with the first finger, the student can ascend into the positions and play major scales on any string through one octave beginning with the first finger.

The major and minor triads with fingering 0-2-0-3-3-0-2-0, 1-3-1-4-4-1-3-1, 2-4-2-1-1-2-4-2 can be introduced early, the latter two in the positions as well. Major scales and triads can also be played on one string with one finger. It is best to integrate scale playing with musical material, so that the student may immediately realize the benefits of scale playing.

Spiccato*

Spiccato bowing has a stimulating effect on young players; furthermore, it is helpful for the development of flexibility and bow balance; this important technique should be introduced early. The slow spiccato and fast spiccato require different techniques and approaches.

The Slow Spiccato

Also called thrown bow, saltando, or artificial spiccato, this bowing can be played at any part of the bow, near the frog in forte, at the balance point (BP) in mezzoforte, at the middle in piano, and occasionally above the middle—even near the tip—when extreme crispness is required. The degree of crispness—percussiveness—is governed by the extent of horizontal and vertical motions; spiccato can be varied from a pin-pointed, high bouncing bow (battuto) to a flaky, smooth stroke that barely leaves the string.

It is best to introduce a free-bouncing, free-moving, live spiccato at first. (See illustration at right.) To get the feel of the bouncing bow, throw the bow repeatedly at the same

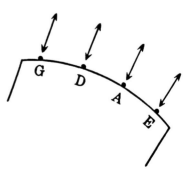

*See also pages 42-43.

spot (near the balance point at first) with a downward motion and without moving the bow horizontally, letting it bounce back on its own. Do this with an uninhibited motion and with a passive feeling in the hand, holding the bow very lightly, on all strings.

Next, combine the horizontal and vertical motions, glancing the bow obliquely with the forearm. The bow will now describe a curve as illustrated by the drawing at the right.

By using more bow (increased horizontal motion), and bouncing it less (decreased vertical motion), a smoother, flaky spiccato can be played, the so-called brushed stroke; in this the bow should be slanted, so that the side hairs will strike the string first.

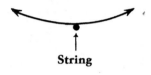

String

In all spiccato bowing it is important that the bow must not be hampered in its movement after hitting the string, but it should jump away from the string quite on its own, due to the elasticity of the bow and string and not because of an extra lifting motion of the hand. Active lifting should be effected on the last notes of spiccato passages or when the notes are quite slow and/or near the frog, where the bow is sluggish. To avoid interference with the natural elasticity of the bow, the grip on the bow should be loose and passive in spiccato.

Experiment first with the slow spiccato on open strings (try also on two open strings in fifths), in even rhythm; after that practice the following rhythmic patterns:

frog: *forte*
BP: *mf*
M: *piano*

Strengthen the up-bow spiccato with the following:

The Fast Spiccato

Also called sautillé, bouncing bow, or natural spiccato, this bowing is derived from the fast détaché or tremolo. Play repeated notes with short bows, shaking the hand in a relaxed manner about the middle—on the string—and gradually move the bow toward the balance point. Move the bow slightly obliquely (moving it rather up and downward and not so much to left and right), keeping the hair flat on the string. At a certain spot of the bow, the bow will begin to bounce, at a lower spot in slower speed and higher in the bow when the notes are faster. The downward impact causes the stick to bite into the string, the stick and hair being close for an instant; immediately after, the tension in the stick relaxes, and the stick moves up from the hair. The hair, fully in contact with the string during the impact, will cease to grip the string at the moment of release, but will not necessarily leave the string. The best effect may be had by allowing some of the hairs to remain on the strings at all times. If the vertical element of the movement is increased, a crisper sound can be produced, and the hairs may actually leave the string. The following rhythmic bowings practiced on open strings—in string crossings, scales, and études—will help to develop the sautillé.

Use the same pitch for each bar:

Do not throw first note.

Playing the sautillé with note repetitions is easy, due to the avoidance of left hand problems. When playing rapid spiccato without note repetitions, the pin-point coordination between fingers and bow is difficult. It is best to practice such passages with the small détaché, first slowly, then fast in small sections. Try for maximum speed in playing short sections of two, three, four, six, eight, twelve, and sixteen notes, whichever numbers are convenient. Slow practicing is helpful for acquiring accuracy, but it will not automatically lead to rapid playing. Fast practicing is important also, and it is best done on short isolated sections at first— then longer ones—to allow control of articulation and intonation.

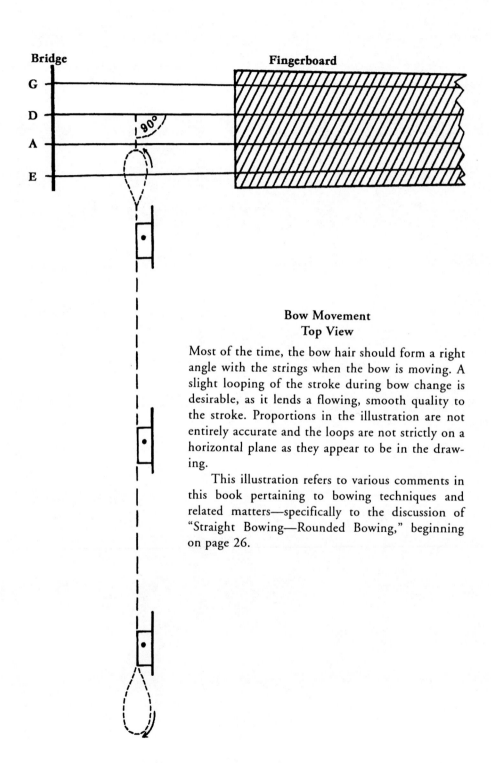

Bridge **Fingerboard**

G
D
A
E

90°

Bow Movement
Top View

Most of the time, the bow hair should form a right angle with the strings when the bow is moving. A slight looping of the stroke during bow change is desirable, as it lends a flowing, smooth quality to the stroke. Proportions in the illustration are not entirely accurate and the loops are not strictly on a horizontal plane as they appear to be in the drawing.

This illustration refers to various comments in this book pertaining to bowing techniques and related matters—specifically to the discussion of "Straight Bowing—Rounded Bowing," beginning on page 26.

Section Two
Violin Teaching
Intermediate—Advanced Levels

More Advanced Shifting

The simplest type of shift is done with the same finger playing in two different positions. This shift is the foundation of the more complicated shifting formulas, as it establishes the actual distances that need to be covered between positions. The string player should practice the simple, distance-measuring shifts over and over, going from one position to any other, carefully judging, measuring, and registering in his mind the actual distance covered, just as a carpenter would measure distances with his tape and ruler. To find a method for identifying the various types of shifts, let's call this simplest type merely a shift. Practice shifts, until you can slide or jump from any one position to any other, on any finger, and in any key with assurance.

In a more complex type of shift, when ascending from a lower finger to a higher one, the "old finger" shifts and measures the distance, and the "new finger" strikes. When descending from a higher to a lower finger, the higher finger shifts and measures the distance, while the lower finger strikes. Let us call this type of shift a "shift-stroke." It is important that in this type of shift we always travel on the "old finger," and articulate well by striking decisively with the "new finger," in order to get a clean, unblurred arrival at the new tone. *In the "shift-stroke" the interval played is always larger than the distance traveled,* and the size of the interval must not create a mental image of an unnecessarily long shift. In elementary teaching and playing it is advisable to keep the "old finger" on the string during the shift (at least in practicing) until it arrives at the new position, thus creating an auxiliary note. In advanced playing this practice is gradually eliminated, and in modern playing the shifts are sounded only when esthetically desirable.

A third type of shift is executed in ascending from a higher to a lower finger. This shift is typical of scale and arpeggio fingerings, when going from the second or third finger to the first finger. This type of shift could be labeled a "shove," since it is characteristic of this shift that the "new finger" (the lower) overtakes the "old finger" (which passively clings to the old spot until the last possible moment), and shoves it out of the way. In the "shove," the shift is felt on the "new finger." In descending, this procedure is insecure, and rather messy

sounding; therefore when descending from a lower to the higher finger, shift on the "old finger," using a "shift-stroke."

A fourth type of shift is the so-called "modern slide," which was forbidden in the first part of the century but gradually gained acceptance. This shift, used only when ascending, is performed with the "new finger"; it is a closer approximation to the vocal portamento than to the other types. It should be done discreetly, with only the last portion of the slide (that immediately below the new pitch) heard faintly.

Anticipated, Delayed Shifts, Change of Bow in Shifts

Regardless of how quickly and skillfully a shift is executed, it still takes time. The time necessary for the shift can be taken either from the first note or from the second note. In the first case we have an "anticipated shift," in the second case a "delayed shift." The "shift-stroke" and the "shift," as a rule are anticipated; the "modern slide" is delayed; the "shove" and even the "shift" can be done either way. When anticipated, the shift is rounder, and is usually allotted a little more time; the delayed shift is done rather quickly.

When a shift is performed with two bow strokes, there is a choice of sliding on the old or on the new bow. Traditionally, the "shift" and the "shift-stroke" were performed on the old bow. Ševčík, however, recommends the "shift" on the new bow; Kreisler also makes most of his "shift-strokes" on the new bow. The "shove" and "modern slide" should always be made on the new bow. The latter one is easier on the up-bow than on the down; as a rule it is easier to camouflage shifts neatly at the tip than at the frog.

Technical Shift and Portamento

When a shift is made due to necessity or convenience, rather than for a musical effect, it should be inconspicuous (the in-between pitches not heard); such a shift is usually labeled a "technical shift."

In singing movements, and whenever a shift is featured for its esthetic quality, it can be played audibly for its particular effect, much as in singing. Such a shift, or rather "slide," is called "portamento." If used discreetly and with moderation, portamento will enhance the performance; otherwise it can be quite repulsive.

Anticipation of the Technical Movement

When shifting after rests or between separated notes, the shifting movement is done with a single motion, decisively and quickly. In legato playing, too sudden and jerky motions during shifts should be avoided. In playing the portamento, the inertia of the arm, resting in one position, should be overcome by anticipating the shift in the arm, and following it up in the hand and fingers. The arm *leads* the shift by leaning in the direction of the new position; the wrist slightly leans in the same direction, and finally the resisting finger follows.

In quick technical shifts, lightness of the movement should be cultivated. To minimize friction during the shift, the motion is anticipated with a release of finger and thumb pressure, as if the finger would be lifted out of the string. During the shift, the thumb glides with a minimum of friction along the neck (which must be extremely smooth and clean), and at the conclusion of the shift the string is again secured by the finger pressure, which is then opposed by the thumb.

The correct timing of anticipating movements is just as important in violin playing as in sports (tennis, golf, etc.). The preparation, the knowing-where-to-go, the "wind-up" must be smoothly followed by the main action without a break, just as exhalation follows inhalation.

Materials for Shifting

The simplest and most obvious materials for shifting are the various intervals played with slurred as well as separate bows. Connect the first position with all the others, using the various types of shifts as described above. Practice major and minor triads on one finger; proceed with the one octave, one string scale, the Ševčík row of arpeggios (Ševčík: Op. 1, Bk. 3), and the Op. 8 of Ševčík; three octave arpeggios also offer good shifting opportunities. Gaylord Yost's book of shifts is helpful. The student should keep in mind that shifting motions (like bowing motions) need countless repetition before they become secure and automatic, and while bowing motions are always present in the literature, shifting motions are rather sparingly used. Therefore shifting technique must be developed with supplementary exercises and by practicing this important technique for a long, long time.

Straight Bowing—Rounded Bowing

For an even tone and steady contact point, the bow must travel in a straight line with the hair forming a right angle to the string. When changing the bow, a slight looping of the movement is desirable to obtain a smooth, flowing stroke.*

However, strokes are also more or less curved around the fulcrum formed by the contact point of bow and string. *This means that the imaginary angle between bow and floor constantly changes during every stroke,* the curve being considerable in string crossings, and slight when playing on a single string.

The cultured bow arm describes flowing, smooth, curved patterns at all times. The principle of straight bowing and "parallelism" merely establishes the need for keeping the hair at a right angle to the strings most of the time and is not in conflict with the roundness of bowing motions.

*Refer to illustration and note, "Bow Movement," on page 22.

In string bowing, sports, and everyday actions, angular, spasmodic motions should be avoided. Stiff, grotesque motions are due to one or more of the following:

Abrupt start and stopping of a motion. Like an automobile starting in low gear, arm motion should also be started with a slow anticipation in which the upper parts lead, while the lower parts and finally the bow follow. Even a fast-moving martelé stroke is anticipated with a minute motion of the upper arm which overcomes the inertia of the resting arm. A motion should not be arrested as if hitting a brick wall but should be allowed to lose its momentum gradually.

Abrupt reversal of direction of the motion. If a motion is reversed and is traced back exactly along the same track, it comes to a complete stop before turning back. When coming to the end of a stroke, the arm must not be suddenly grabbed with the muscles of the shoulder and upper arm, then reversed; instead, motions should be reversed with curved or with pendulum-like movement. Pendulum-like motions have graduated speeds; they start almost imperceptibly, increase speed, and finally slow down to a complete halt. If a pendulum is deflected sideways in its motion at one end, an elliptical movement will result; if it is deflected at both ends in opposite direction, a "figure 8" pattern will result. The pendulum motion, the elliptical, and the figure 8 patterns are all natural flowing motions, as can easily be tested with a freely swinging arm. Unfortunately, the pendulum motion is not too suitable for bowing, and it is the elliptical and the figure 8 motions that allow a smooth, flowing, continuous stroke. In these, the arm (or any portion of it) does not come to a stop; every motion is gently deflected at the end and flows without a break into the next.

These flowing, curved motions are utilized not only in string playing but also in other actions, for instance, conducting. A 2/4 meter is not conducted with angular, down and up motions:

but rather like this:

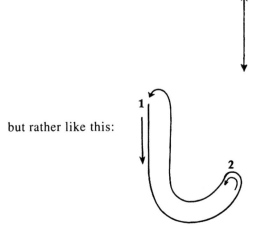

In 3/4 time we do not beat a triangle:

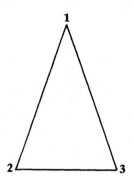

but rather:

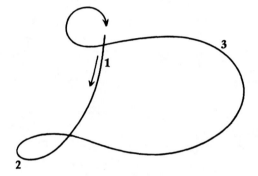

Abrupt, angular change of direction of a motion. Motions should be rounded, not angular. In string crossings, the change of string level should be performed with an anticipated, curved motion, instead of an angular, broken line. (See pages 10-11.)

The Size and Direction of Rounded Bowings

The size of the curve (the deviation of the stroke from the straight center line (see illustration, p. 29) is determined by the boundaries of the next string, the speed of the stroke, and the spot on the bow (proximity to tip or frog). It is advantageous to use somewhat larger curves in slow strokes, since the added bowing room relieves restriction and allows a freer movement. In fast playing, on the other hand, excessive motion should be avoided. The curves are wider at the tip than at the frog and are much wider in string crossing than when playing on a single string.

The elliptical and figure 8 patterns can run in clockwise or in counter-clockwise direction. The string crossing always determines the direction of the curve, but when playing on one string the choice of direction is up to the player. The counterclockwise elliptical figure tends to lay the bow more firmly on the string at the tip, due to the continuous pronation of the arm through the change at the tip. The clockwise curve at the tip lightens the pressure at the moment of change, and tends to articulate, rather than to sustain the stroke. The clockwise elliptical curve feels more natural in rapid strokes, especially in sautillé. However, no definite rules can be laid down concerning the direction of the curves; they are interchangeable (with the exception of string crossing), and should be done in the most natural manner. One need not be aware at all times of the direction of the curves, but in case of some bowing difficulties (especially before and after string crossing), recognition of the most convenient looping motion will often bring surprisingly quick results.

The figure 8 curve is the best for sustained strokes; it tends to equalize down- and up-bows and permits maximum weaving around the center-line in the case of slow sustained strokes.

The curves and loops appearing in the bow also appear in the arm, a fact often ignored because of the small motion in the upper arm. For a well-coordinated motion, the whole arm must be supple, sensitively balanced, so that it may swing freely in all directions. The upper arm leads in slow strokes and also gives whip-like impulses in fast strokes.

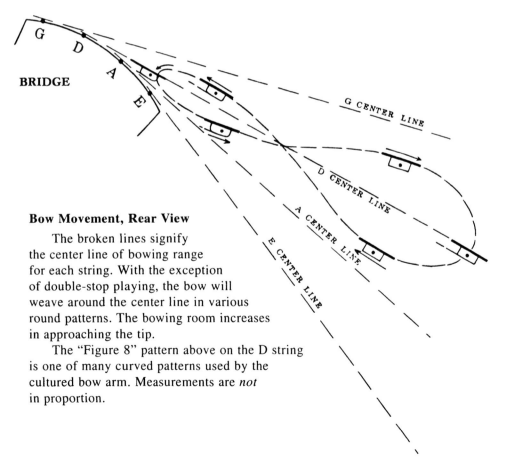

Bow Movement, Rear View

The broken lines signify the center line of bowing range for each string. With the exception of double-stop playing, the bow will weave around the center line in various round patterns. The bowing room increases in approaching the tip.

The "Figure 8" pattern above on the D string is one of many curved patterns used by the cultured bow arm. Measurements are *not* in proportion.

The Most Frequent Bowing Patterns

The curves describe the movement of the thumb–middle finger axis. These curves, though much smaller in size and slightly off in phase, are also produced by the movement of any given spot on the elbow.

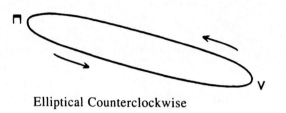

Elliptical Counterclockwise

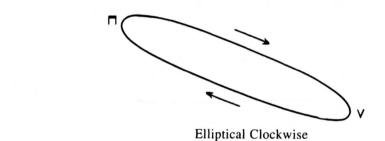

Elliptical Clockwise

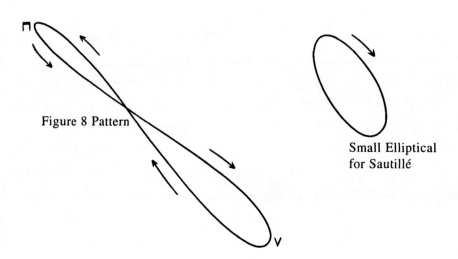

Figure 8 Pattern

Small Elliptical
for Sautillé

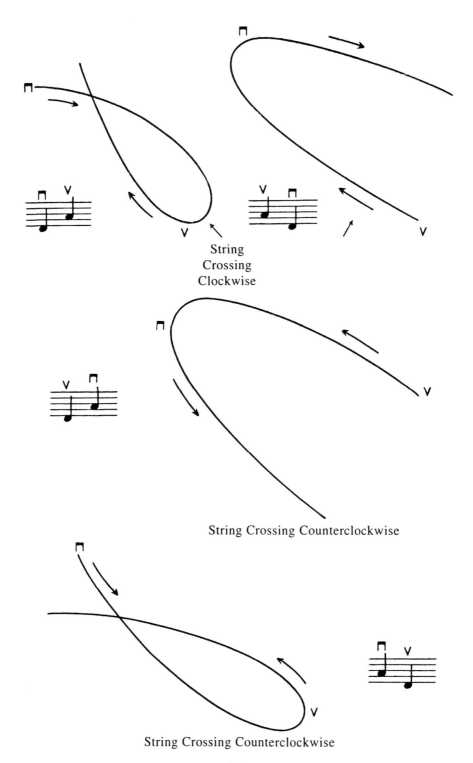

String
Crossing
Clockwise

String Crossing Counterclockwise

String Crossing Counterclockwise

Bow Pressure, Leverage

With the free rolling motion of the arm, a most advantageous leverage may be obtained so that the pressure needed at the tip or in *forte* will not be felt as a strain in the fingers. Thus the pressure is produced with a relatively passive feeling in the hand, and with a rolling motion of the arm that turns the first finger against the top of the stick, while the elbow very slightly rises with a small counterclockwise motion (positive pressure). In relaxing the bow pressure, the arm rolls downward, releasing the pressure of the first finger from the top of the bow (shifting its contact to the side of the bow), and bringing the ring and little fingers into stronger contact with the stick, while the elbow very slightly turns toward the floor (negative pressure). The inside curving (concave) of the stroke aids pressure, while the outward (convex) curve relaxes pressure.

In addition to the above-mentioned finger, hand, and arm activity, there is a strong feeling of pull in the fingers during sustained, tense strokes, which reverses with the direction of the stroke. During down-bows, the pulling pressure of the fingers causes the hand knuckles to give a little (they flatten); the fingers are curved and more obtuse, while in up-bows the first finger leans well against the stick, the fingers straighten themselves slightly and are more oblique, and the hand knuckles give in the opposite direction, becoming slightly more protruding. The main body of the pressure should not come from the fingers, which are transmitting and refining agents. The fingers should not be unduly spread on the bow for the sake of greater leverage; instead, the whole arm should be used as a cantilever, with the shoulder joint serving as a fulcrum.

Tone Quality—Physical Factors

The development of a beautiful string tone is probably the greatest single success factor in string performance and study. In the final analysis, good string tone is determined by conditions existing at the contact point of string and bow, and string and fingers (left).

Determining factors of good tone quality are:

(1) Proper selection of the contact point between bow and string (CP), its exact location between bridge and fingerboard.

(2) The speed of the bow as it moves across the string (the amount of hair that passes through the contact point in a given length of time).

(3) The pressure of the bow at the CP, i.e., the amount of pressure received by the string. A sufficient amount of pressure is needed at the CP to provide enough friction to grip and move the string from its resting position. (Rosin is also needed to provide friction; too much rosin, however, arrests the string in its free motion, like too much pressure, and causes unpleasant surface noises.)

(4) The tension of the stroke, or the proportion of the bow speed and bow pressure.

(5) The amount of hair in contact with the string (cant), and the tension of the stick.

(6) Articulation of fingers and bow. The quality of the attack, duration and release of the stroke, finger application.

(7) Vibrato.

(8) The adjustments and the accessories of the instrument.

(9) The acoustical properties of the room, and its relative humidity. This latter condition, being somewhat beyond control, will not be discussed. The other factors will be taken up in order.

The Contact Point

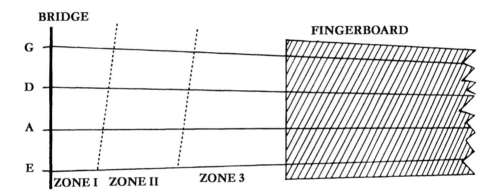

ZONE* I. *For long, sustained strokes and loud playing.* In the vicinity of the bridge (Zone I) the string is stiff and will not respond to a light touch of the bow unless the bow speed is quite slow. The bow pressure should be rather strong in order to set the string into vibration.

With the contact point remaining the same, the pressure is proportionate with the bow speed, i.e., when the bow moves slowly, only a moderate amount of pressure is needed, which should be increased when the bow picks up speed. However, the bow speed is necessarily limited in Zone I, since a fast-moving bow will produce surface tones. The "sul ponticello" effect is produced by light and swift strokes near the bridge, setting the upper partials into vibration without sufficient vibration of the fundamental pitch of the string.

ZONE II. *For normal playing conditions.* In a medium position between bridge and fingerboard the bow can be moved fairly fast with medium to high pressure (loud), or slowly, with low or medium pressure. This zone is most suitable for average playing conditions and therefore is the logical spot for most of the playing, especially on the elementary level.

*The zone division is an arbitrary measure for the illustration of the diversity of the contact point. There are no distinct border lines between the zones, the dividing dotted lines being approximate and fictitious.

ZONE III. *For soft playing and for swiftly moving light bows.* Near the fingerboard the string is resilient, responds easily, and lends itself to light, effortless playing. Here the string is weak and collapses easily under bow pressure; for this reason, the fingerboard area is not suitable for heavy and slowly moving strokes.

Timbre and Contact Point

When playing in Zone I, the high partials of the string are favored and the tone has a brilliant and intense, oboe-like quality. If the relationship of bow speed and bow pressure is disproportionate (not enough pressure), a thin, shrill tone quality will result. On the other hand, if the pressure is too great, the tone will be smothered. In sustained tones with sufficient pressure, a rich, full tone can be obtained due to the wide range of overtones in Zone I.

In Zone II, the tone is neither too brilliant nor too mellow but has a full round quality, somewhat similar to the clarinet tone. The full singing quality is the most desirable normal sound of the violin.

In Zone III, the tone has a flute-like, velvety quality (flautando); soft and mellow, it lends itself to beautiful effects in *dolce-semplice,* lullaby-like passages. The ease of playing and the charm of this effect, however, should not make the player overly indulgent in this type of tone production which, if used too often, lends an effeminate, powerless quality to the performance. The mellow, somewhat dull and hazy quality is due to the dominance of the fundamental tone at the expense of the upper partials.

Shifting the Contact Point

The contact point must be steady when notes of even quality are played, and the bow hair must cross the string at a right angle (parallelism). Poor direction of the bow stroke will cause constant shifting of the CP, resulting in a bad, haphazardly changing tone quality. A typical fault is the backward-moving downbow, resulting in a drift of the CP toward the fingerboard, and the forward-pushed up-bow, with the bow pointing toward the left ear and a corresponding shift of the CP toward the fingerboard when coming toward the frog. For an even tone quality, the bow arm should be disciplined to strict observance of parallelism, which will then result in a steady contact point.

Much of the time, however, a change in the CP is a must. The CP is influenced by the various strings. The lower strings are less responsive near the bridge; therefore, the CP generally shifts toward the fingerboard when playing on them. In general, the higher the string, the closer the contact point should be to the bridge.

The CP is also dependent upon the string length. In the higher positions, it is closer to the bridge; high notes often suffer by nonobservance of this rule. When leaping up to a high note, a considerable drift (toward the bridge) of the CP is necessary. A reversed drift is needed in long downward leaps. The CP also changes with the dynamics, as discussed above.

The Speed of the Bow

As a rule, use as much bow on each note as possible within the limit of feasibility. The volume of tone is much more dependent on bow speed than on bow pressure. Greater bow speed lessens the tension of the stroke and, in general, results in a freer style of bowing.

The bow speed is generally greater on the higher strings and in the higher positions. The heavier strings require more pressure and a somewhat restricted bow speed. In the following example, use more bow on the high notes than on the low ones.

Less Bow   **More Bow**   **Less Bow**

When playing high notes on the E string, use a generous amount of bow and change the bow on long slurred strokes. This short and weak string will take only a limited amount of bow pressure.

Sustained Strokes

The slower the stroke, the less pressure will be tolerated by the string at a given contact point. Therefore, with the slowing down of the stroke, the CP should be shifted toward the bridge—unless a softer tone is desired. The opposite is also true: the faster the stroke, the more pressure may be applied at a given CP, resulting in a louder tone. If no increase in volume is desired, the CP must be shifted toward the fingerboard in faster strokes.

In slow strokes, tone production is critical, and a very strict relationship of contact point, bow speed, and bow pressure is necessary. Even slight errors will damage the tone. The fingers should embrace the bow with greater intensity and control the passage and pressure of the bow with care. In sustained strokes, the tension of the hand is much greater, giving a sensation of a slow "pull," with the fingers resisting the passage of the bow as if trying to move in the opposite direction of the stroke. In these slow pulled strokes (which are the key to tone production in slow movements), the fingers are slightly more curved in down-bows than in up-bows.

Fluent Strokes

With fairly swift passage of the bow, slight errors in the relation of contact point—bow speed—pressure will not affect the tone to a great extent, and the tension of the stroke and that of the hand is diminished. For this reason, swiftly moving, rapid and fluent strokes should be cultivated with the beginning student for some time before turning to sustained tones. Lively moving strokes are both easier and better liked in the early stages. (Repeated notes will allow fast strokes without creating intonation and coordination problems for the left hand.)

Bow Pressure

In dealing with pressure we should distinguish between pressure applied to the bow (human pressure) and that received by the string. For instance, if we lay the bow on the string at the balance point, approximately two ounces of natural weight will be received by the string. Now, if we move the bow to the tip without adding pressure upon the bow, the natural weight of the bow being transmitted to the string will be less than one ounce (the bow being supported in large part by the thumb). In order to supplement the lost bow pressure, human pressure should be applied to the bow. To regain the lost pressure (a little over one ounce), almost two pounds of human pressure must be applied upon the bow, because of the disadvantageous leverage that exists when playing at the tip.

In the following, only the pressure received by the string will be discussed, and not human pressure applied by the performer.

As mentioned above, enough pressure is required at the contact point to make the string adhere to the bow hair when drawing the bow. If the pressure is insufficient, the hair will pass over without taking hold of the string, and move it to the limit of its resiliency. This is the cause of a thin surface tone in which the overtones dominate without sufficient vibration of the string fundamental. On the other hand, if too much pressure is applied, the hair arrests the string and prevents it from vibrating freely, thus causing a dull, often scratchy tone. The over-pressed and under-pressed bow are pitfalls of tone production, and their peculiar sound effect should be immediately noticed and remedied by the player.

Bow Pressure and Dynamics

Increased pressure has less effect upon the dynamics than is generally believed. It is the quality (timbre) of the tone that changes considerably with increased pressure and increased tension in the stroke. With increased pressure and closer contact point to the bridge, a richer, brighter tone can be produced, one that has the full spectrum of the upper partials. On the other hand, strokes with a minimum of bow pressure are played nearer the fingerboard and produce a sound in which the fundamental pitch dominates. This sound is mellower, flute-like, lacks strength and brilliance, and is somewhat similar in quality to harmonics.

In artistic performance both the brilliant and mellow qualities are employed and are desirable; even in a school orchestra, surprising tonal effects can be produced by purposeful deviation from the normal sounds.

Bow Pressure and Pitch Range

The thicker strings require and tolerate greater bow pressure. The lower strings, being thicker, require more pressure than the upper strings. The E string, especially, sounds forced under a heavy bow. Metal strings require more pressure and produce a more hollow, less intense tone. It is unwise to combine metal-core D and G strings with a gut or aluminum-wound gut A

36

string. If metal strings are preferred, due to financial and climatic reasons, use only the best grades, those with flat wire ribbons. Metal strings, however, do not respond as well to a light touch of the bow and are much restricted in their timbre variations.

The bow pressure also varies with the string length. The shorter the string length, the less pressure will be tolerated. Therefore, when in the high positions, especially on the E string, play with relatively light pressure.

In playing double stops, only half of the total bow pressure is received by each string; therefore the pressure tolerance of the strings at a given contact point is doubled. If the pressure is not increased, the CP must be nearer to the fingerboard. The same is true in chord playing, only more so.

Changing Dynamics

Greater bow speed and pressure and a contact point closer to the bridge will increase volume; their opposites will decrease it. Yet, if a satisfactory sound is achieved and then the pressure is increased in an effort to produce more volume, the tone will crack. Similarly, increasing the speed of the bow at the same contact point will result in a surface tone, as will moving the bow closer to the bridge.

The triumvirate of bow speed–pressure–contact point is such that a good tone will result only with a specific constellation of all three factors. A good tone is the evidence of correct proportions, and if we change one of these three factors, the tone will necessarily be spoiled. It is therefore erroneous to believe that a crescendo can be produced by increasing the pressure or the speed of the bow alone, or by simply moving the bow closer to the bridge.

When changing dynamics, at least two of the three factors must be changed simultaneously to maintain a good tone quality.

A crescendo may be obtained by the following formulas: (a) increase bow speed *and* bow pressure; (b) draw bow closer to the bridge *and* increase bow pressure; (c) increase bow speed, pressure and move contact point closer to bridge.

A diminuendo may be obtained the following ways: (a) move the bow toward fingerboard *and* decrease pressure; (b) slow down bow *and* decrease pressure; (c) slow down bow, decrease pressure, and move closer to fingerboard. Use (c) for maximum effect.

In playing the last note of a phrase it is natural to taper the tone. Beginners will enjoy the "finish" that comes to the playing with a nice diminuendo effect at the end of a phrase. This can best be done by slowing the bow as it approaches the tip, simultaneously shifting the balance of the hand from the first to the third and fourth fingers (supination), and by letting the bow drift toward the fingerboard.

Tension of the Stroke

The tension of the stroke is not synonymous with loudness, nor does it mean stiffness. An intense *piano* can be played with a slowly moving bow and relatively high pressure near the bridge. Strong control, more active finger work, and well-sustained intensity are the earmarks of a high-tensioned stroke, produced by a relatively slow-moving bow stroke.

A tense stroke can be recognized best by its intense, reedy quality, both in *piano* and *forte*. The greater the bow pressure and the slower the stroke, the higher is the tension. Bow speed reduces tension. The higher the tension, the closer is the contact point to the bridge.

Musical Expression and Related Tone Quality

Effective expression of the character of music can be enhanced by the right choice of tone quality and bowing. This character or type of expression is often identified by the following terminology:

Semplice: Simple, unaffected; play with light bows, avoid excessive vibrato.

Dolce: A gentle, sweet effect; play with flowing, relaxed light bows, rather softly, with velvety flute-like tone quality, near the fingerboard. Avoid excessive vibrato and tension.

Cantabile: Singing tone, arioso: play with full open tone, use vibrato freely.

Espressivo: With expression; play with intense, high-tensioned stroke, well projected, bring out details, nuances; use vibrato. Usually played with a full tone, unless marked *p. espr.*

Sotto voce: Soft, yet dramatic and intense; play with a high-tensioned stroke, yet very softly; use vibrato.

Risoluto: Resolute, determined, bold; play with energetic, accented strokes, and with a strong tone.

The Slanting of the Bow

The tone quality also depends on the amount of hair contacting the string. If the bow is too heavily haired, the strings will not vibrate freely; surface noises and a dull tone will result, due to absorption of the upper partials. If the hair is too thin, a clear (but often thin), glassy sound will result.

Similarly, the quality of the tone can be altered by the player by consciously changing the cant of the bow. In soft playing, the bow should be slanted as a rule to reduce surface noises, which are not sufficiently masked by the low volume. In loud playing, the surface noises are not as noticeable when playing with the full width of the hair. When playing with a narrow ribbon of the hair, the high partials are favored, making the tone more brilliant; with a wider ribbon, the tone is mellower. For this reason, in high positions and for harmonics less hair should be used. As a rule more hair should be used on the low strings than on the high strings.

The cant of the hair also has a bearing on the smoothness of the stroke. When the hair is flat on the string with the stick vertically over it, the bow is taut, springy, and bounces easily during its passage unless it is pressed into the string firmly, which should be done only in loud playing. In light playing (without sufficient pressure), the stroke is rough when using the full hair, and the bow tends to bounce.

The hair is stiff near the frog, and for this reason it is advisable to play at the frog with a well-slanted bow for flexibility of tone and also for eliminating the pressure, which is superfluous at the frog. It is wise to increase the cant of the hair when approaching the frog and to flatten it when moving away from it. In order to play with a desirable, strong tone, the student, however, should use full hair most of the time.

Articulation, Left Hand

In evaluating a musical tone we are especially sensitive to the quality of its beginning and ending. The beginning and ending of each note come under the heading of "articulation," and this aspect of tone production, directly related to the clarity and neatness of playing, is determined by the action of fingers (left hand), as well as the bow.

Left Hand Fingers

Articulation of the fingers will be discussed first.

The open string is known for its bright, hard quality. A similar quality could be produced on stopped tones, if we were to put a thimble on the fretting finger. If the finger is applied with very strong pressure, however, a somewhat similar quality may be obtained. The strong pressure hardens the fingertips, and the tone quality will become harder, sometimes even glassy. Reducing the pressure results in a mellower tone, and with further relaxation of the pressure, the tone gets blurred, indistinct. Hence, the quality of the tone is influenced by the method of finger application, which can vary from brittle through normal to blurred. The shape and fleshiness of the fingertips also have considerable influence on the articulation, and those with well padded, yet not too thick fingers, have a definite advantage.

Finger Action

The finger action can be divided into three phases: (1) the finger prepares the stroke and drops to the string; (2) it keeps the string down; (3) it leaves the string.

The fingers should be dropped to the string with a live, spring-like action. A slow initial contact with the string should be avoided because it will blur the beginning of the sound, until the finger "arrives" on the fingerboard, when the sound will improve. Strive for a decisive, clear finger impact that will produce a ringing initial sound. After an articulate impact, relax the finger and allow it to vibrate. In sustained singing tones, the finger should be placed rather than dropped, while in passage work the *ballistic* action of the fingers is used, i.e., an initial thrust, with a relaxed, coasting follow-through. In this second type of finger action, the hand is more relaxed than in the first type, since the pressure is not sustained, thereby increasing the tension of the hand. But in either case, the finger should arrive on the string with sufficient speed to produce a clear, articulate sound. The angle of the finger and, in general, the position of the fingertip influences the tone. The extreme of the fingertip will favor brilliancy of tone; a flatter application will mellow the tone.

The finger pressure following the initial attack has a bearing on the tone. Discarding the possibility of an insufficiently pressed finger that results in a blurred sound (unfortunately, this is often the case, more so when the strings are set too high over the fingerboard), the tone is more brilliant with strong finger pressure, and rather mellow when the pressure is at a minimum.

The release of the string should be instantaneous and springy like the attack; otherwise a blurred quality will result due to the same causes as above. The lifting of the fingers is done against gravity; furthermore, the extensor muscles performing the act are by nature underdeveloped. For this reason there is a greater tendency toward indistinct articulation when the notes are formed by the lifting of fingers (as in descending scales). For articulate finger action, it is well to emphasize the quick, backward motion of the fingers from the knuckles. This will strengthen the extensor muscles. Do not point a lifted finger toward the sky, as this reduces the ability of its neighbor to apply pressure to the string. The finger that follows a lifted finger has a tendency to go along with the latter, instead of performing its duty of holding the string with sufficient power.

When the descending interval played on one string is wide, an increased sluggishness is apparent (probably due to the sudden change in string length), and in such a case, a slight left hand pizzicato, as if scraping the string, is advisable. The need for this action is especially pronounced when descending to the open string, in playing grace notes, and in short trills.

Bow Articulation

While the articulation of the fingers is a relatively simple matter, the area of bow articulation is a complex one. Here we must deal with a great variety of bowings and with nuances of application.

The many types of bowings can be classified into two main categories: *legato types* and *marcato types*. Bowings also can be classified as "on the string" and "off the string" bowings.

Legato Types

Legato bowings are smooth; the tone begins with a soft "touch" of the bow, as if starting with soft consonants—"la" or "ma." The three changes (change of bow, change of string, and change of position) must be done smoothly with rounded motions, avoiding jerkiness and bad accentuation.

When starting the tone, the bow must not grip the string in advance. The stroke should rather begin like a breath, with the pressure applied as the bow moves. This can be accomplished in two ways: (1) by setting the bow in motion before touching the string, then "landing" with the bow very smoothly, or (2) by placing the bow gently with the side hairs on the strings, then starting the motion in the arm with a delayed action of the fingers and wrist, applying the pressure simultaneously with the start of the bow.

Smoothness and lack of abruptness of tone and motion are the earmarks of good legato-type bowings. The various types are:

Son filé (spun tone), is a sustained, "laced" bowing, an intensively pulled singing tone (see also Tension of the Stroke, pages 34-38).

Slurred legato, combines two or more notes played on the same bow.

Articulated legato emphasizes the individual notes, as if tonguing them, for greater expression; used only in moderate speeds.

Singing détaché (sometimes called German détaché) denotes an active, yet smooth bowing, with one note to each bow, usually in eighth- or sixteenth-note values; in this stroke the change of bow is concealed as much as possible. This stroke is the "bread and butter" of the string player, probably the most important of all strokes to master.

Portato (also called louré) denotes slightly separated round notes, usually marked with dashes; one or more notes on each stroke.

Espressivo, cantabile, dolce, and *amabile* are usually associated with legato bowing.

Marcato Types

In contrast to the preceding, marcato-type bowings are more or less hard, brisk, and well accentuated. The tone beginning in marcato bowings can be compared to the hard consonants—"ta" or "pa," etc. Marcato-type bowings are usually short; the bow is pushed rather than pulled with a ballistic action of the arm, making an instantaneous thrust on each note, then relaxed with the bow permitted to coast after the attack. These bowings lend vigor, fire, and zest, the masculine elements of the performance, and should therefore be cultivated. The specific bowings in this group are:

Martelé (hammered stroke—the adjective denotes the sound effect, not the movement). In this bowing the string is firmly held with the hair in advance; then the bow is quickly pushed with a simultaneous release of a good portion of the pressure. The bow should arrive at a sudden stop and simultaneously grip the string in preparation for the next note. Due to the hard, explosive beginning of the martelé (begins with a "pop"), which necessitates the placement of the bow on the string in advance, the speed of a genuine martelé is limited. When a vibrant tone does not come to an abrupt end following the attack, the stroke is called "martelé chanté" or singing martelé. When the speed is too great for the preparation of a genuine "popping" attack, the stroke transforms itself into:

Accented détaché (sometimes called French détaché). This is similar to the détaché above, except the bow changes here are not concealed but rather emphasized with the accents. This is a brilliant, buoyant stroke, which develops clarity of articulation. When played with exceedingly short bows, yet with very strong accents, this bowing is sometimes called "serré"—crowded. This is a very good practice bowing that develops coordination between fingers and bow, as well as accentuation. To correct a spineless, blurred détaché, practice the "serré" bowing.

Piqué is a tiny biting stroke—the attack of a martelé without the stroke. It is used for the shortest staccato notes if they are not too fast, but more often it is used as a preparatory practice stroke for the martelé and slow spiccato. Here the bow is "glued" to the string first (*collé*), then is suddenly released and moved a tiny bit, releasing the pressure simultaneously. The movement is done mostly with the fingers and is therefore a fine stroke to develop finger control and flexibility. Practice it in any part of the bow, producing a tiny, clear and explosive bell-like effect. (See pg. 16.)

Staccato has a double meaning—it is a general term for all short notes, regardless of how they are produced; as a specific term for the string player, it denotes two or more martelé notes taken on the same bow. The martelé-staccato sounds much like the martelé; it is not too fast, with not too many notes taken on the same bow. The rapid-staccato is a reflex-like, repetitive action of the bow, producing a machine-gun-like effect, with a series of notes in one bow, played usually as fast as possible.

Dotted rhythms, the rapid dotted eighth with the sixteenth, or the dotted sixteenth with the thirty-second, should be played as two successive accented détaché notes followed by a rest. According to Leopold Mozart, the dotted note should be prolonged, and the short note played as quickly as possible. In fast tempo, both notes are played as short as possible, compensating with a rest between the notes. The bow should be stopped after the dotted note, but not before it. In slow tempi, the proper ratio between the note values must be observed, early music excepted.

Other "On the String" Bowings

All of the preceding bowings are played on the string "à la corde." Other on-the-string bowings that have no legato or marcato character are:

Rapid détaché. One of the most frequent bowings, played with short, rapidly changing bows, mostly above the middle of the bow.

Sautillé (French) or *rapid spiccato* (Italian). Also called natural spiccato, bouncing bow. It is played much the same way as the rapid détaché, but with a stroke that has a slightly oblique angle to the direction of the stick. The

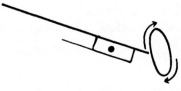

The Direction of the Bow Stroke
in Rapid Détaché

The Direction of the Bow Stroke
in Sautillé

downward flipping of the bow brings out resistance in the elastic stick, which wants to bounce off the string. If the vertical factor of the stroke is considerable, the bow will leave the string; if it is mild, only part of the hairs will leave the string, yet the beating of the stick will create a crisp spiccato-like effect.

The bouncing of the bow will take place in a limited area of the bow— around the balance point in moderate speed, and around the middle if fast.

Tremolo is a fast, repetitious stroke played with a shaking motion of the hand near the tip when soft, and at the middle when loud. Long-lasting, tiresome tremolos at the tip can be facilitated by turning the stick toward the bridge.

"Off the String" Bowings

In this family of bowings, the bow may be first placed, then lifted off the string, or it may be thrown on the string, then jump up by itself.

Spiccato (Italian), also called saltando, artificial spiccato, thrown bow. There are two main types of spiccato, the slow and the fast. The slow spiccato is a thrown bow in which the bow is glanced against the string, then after meeting the resistance of the string, the bow is kicked back. It can be played in any part of the bow, unlike the fast spiccato (sautillé), which can only be played in a limited area of the bow.

The slow spiccato is played near the frog in *forte,* and higher up on the bow in softer passages. Depending upon the angle of glancing, the sound may be quite crisp, or flaky, even brushed, barely leaving the string. If high up on the bow, the sound will be very pointed and hard, whereas when played with the soft parts of the hair (especially if slanted), a fine silky quality may be obtained. In the slow spiccato, each note is formed with a voluntary action of the bow arm. The down-bow is aided by gravity, but the up-bow must be energized to equal its impact on the string.

The fast spiccato or sautillé (discussed earlier) may be on or off the string. Here the up-bows are involuntary rebounding actions, and there is a sensation of shaking the hand in groups of notes instead of moving it separately on every single note.

Staccato volante, or flying staccato, signifies two or more bouncing notes taken on one up-bow. In moderate speed it is best done around the middle third of the bow, if fast, with the third fourth of the bow; and if slow and louder, nearer the frog. Every note is coaxed with an upward kick of the hand to overcome gravity.

Ricochet, also called *jeté* or thrown staccato, creates a snare drum effect. Usually taken on the down-bow, only the first note is given an initial thrust, and the notes that follow (only a few) rebound on their own.

Piqué (described earlier) can be also classified as a lifted stroke. Practice it with any part of the bow, then jump from one spot to another, always producing a clear, biting sound.

Rebound* is a very useful stroke. In this, the bow is moved and

---

*So named by the writer.

returned in the air to the point of origin. It can be performed with martelé or portato-like strokes, moving, lifting, and returning the bow with a single rounded motion. This is an excellent bowing to coordinate the motions of the upper arm, forearm, hand, fingers, and bow.

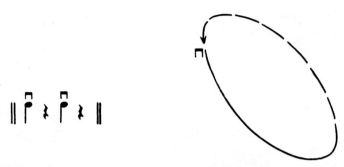

This bowing is also done fast at the frog with repeated down-bows, a powerful hammer effect, or with repeated up-bows, a graceful light stroke in the lower portion of the bow. Repeated down-bow chords are also played with the same stroke.

Accentuation

Accents help to give meaning and clarity to the musical performance. It is due to accentuation that we can feel the meter and the rhythm. Also, with a few well-placed accents, the phrasing and musical idea may be better realized.

There are two kinds of accents—metric accents, and occasional or expressive accents. The first type is in the service of the meter, of the rhythmic pulse of music; the latter is used to give emphasis to the important notes of the phrase.

In practice, accents are accomplished by various means. At times the emphasized note is simply played a little louder than its partners (think of "Lightly Row"—where the first note of the first, second, and fourth bar are a little louder than the others). Other times, the emphasized note has an explosive character and the bow bites into the string. For such brisk accents, the bow must firmly grip the string, then move with a partial release of the pressure, as in the martelé. In expressive, singing movements, the so-called "pressure accent" is used. Here the bow does not bite into the string, but a round accent is produced by a momentary increase of pressure and bow speed. The stick is gently bent with a simultaneous increase of speed. A more intensive vibrato concurrent with the accent can crown the effect.

The "agogic accent" is a stress (tenuto) obtained by slight prolonging of the note; this effect should be used sparingly.

44

Vibrato

The Physical Properties of the Vibrato*

The string instrument vibrato is a periodical and small change of pitch and intensity. The "pitch vibrato" is controlled by the player. The "intensity vibrato" is a by-product of the vibrato movement and is also due to the resonance of the strings. Since "intensity vibrato" is not controlled by the player, it will not be discussed further.

The properties of the vibrato are regularity, amplitude, and speed. Lack of *regularity* is the most common cause of faulty vibrato and is responsible for some feeble effects produced by the poor player. Lack of a coordinated vibrato motion and stiffening are responsible for the irregular movement.

The *speed* (rate) of the average artistic vibrato motion is just under seven cycles per second, one cycle being a back and forward motion. In actual playing, the rate will vary from about five to nine cycles per second. The speed can be clocked with a metronome. Vibrate in the half position, knocking the back of the hand against the peg. Taking four knocks as one beat, find the corresponding metronome speed. Let's suppose that the metronome is matched at 90 beats per second; the total number of vibrato motions then would be 360 in one minute, or six motions in one second. While this speed is sufficiently high to produce a good vibrato, it is below the artistic average. To get a speed of seven cycles per second, the metronome should be set at 105 (104), with four motions falling on each beat; for eight motions per second, the metronome setting should be 120.

However, the student should not be so much concerned about the speed as he should be about the other two factors of the vibrato which are of greater importance. One should especially be careful of forcing the vibrato speed at the expense of stiff arm muscles.

The *amplitude* is the most variable factor of vibrato, the variations depending on dynamics. In loud playing the amplitude, or extent, is greater than in soft tones. A vibrato motion that sounds acceptable in *forte* may sound nauseatingly wide in *piano*. And a pleasing vibrato in *pianissimo* may not be noticed at all in *forte*.

More often than not, faulty vibratos have too wide an amplitude, although a stiff arm and pinching fingers tend to produce a tight, too narrow and bleating effect, which also hinders the player when playing *forte-cantilena*.

The Vibrato Movement

The vibrato movement should be a free, coordinated oscillation of the hand, similar to the motion of the bow arm when playing the rapid détaché, sautillé, or tremolo. Somewhat similar, but slower motions are made quite naturally in everyday life, such as waving goodbye, tapping with a pencil, or petting a dog. A good vibrato is not produced by a local motion of the hand

---

* Seashore, Emil. *The Vibrato: University of Iowa Studies in the Psychology of Music.* Iowa City, Vol. 1, 1932.

from the wrist, but is a coordinated oscillation in which the back and forward motions of the hand are balanced by a slight rolling motion of the upper arm.

To establish a free, coordinated vibrato motion, practice first without the instrument. Hold both hands out in front at arm length, with palms down, index fingertip and thumb touching; now shake the hand up and down with a narrow extent, keeping the wrist and forearm on a fairly straight line, but not rigid. Now turn the two palms toward one another, and continue the shaking motion on a horizontal plane; finally turn the hands toward the face and continue the shaking motion. Right-handed persons will find the motion easier for that hand, and should try to improve their left-hand motion until it approximates the skill of the other hand. Practice the shaking of the hand in the three positions above, and in rhythmic groups of 2, 3, 4, 6, 8, 9, 12, and 16 motions, each group four times.

When a free, balanced shake of the left hand is established,* apply the same motion to the violin. Hold violin in banjo position, and place the thumb against the neck, with the base of first finger close to the opposite side of the neck, but without gripping it. Relax arm, have a feeling of hanging the arm on the neck (drop arm occasionally to keep it free and relaxed), then shake the hand with a similar motion as before. Repeat the action with the violin in "shotgun" position (set against the right armpit), finally in the regular position. Practice the motion in rhythmic groups as before. If a poor, uncoordinated vibrato motion becomes a habit, it is interesting to note how the motion changes when moving the violin from the right to the left shoulder; it takes time to re-educate a conditioned reflex to assume new ways of operation.

When the motion becomes natural with the fingers off the string, proceed by placing the second or third finger on the string, but barely touching it. Gradually increase the pressure as you practice the vibrato motion in rhythmic groups as before, and in three places: in banjo position, with the violin against the right shoulder, and in playing position.

All of the preceding are to be practiced without the bow. When the motion becomes natural enough, practice separated and repeated quarter notes with the bow, with vibrato, in scales and études; then proceed with longer notes.

These exercises should give a good start to the vibrato in a few weeks. Vibrato studies that will aid further development include those by Carl Flesch, Louis Stoelzing, Gilbert Waller, and Valborg Leland's *The Dounis Principles of Violin Playing.***

*Synchronized with the motion of the hand, there is a slight involuntary rolling motion in the upper arm, and when the movement is performed in playing position, this slight roll brings out a tiny sideways motion in the elbow, to the left with the forward motion of the hand, and to the right with the backward motion of the hand.

**Reference should he made to the MENC publication *Music Education Materials — a Selected Bibliography* for suggestions of books and other materials.

The Adjustments and Accessories of the Instrument

The owner of an automobile will have his car regularly serviced and checked to keep it in good condition. The violin is also a sensitive instrument which needs regular servicing and care. Even the best violin will sound poorly without adequate equipment and adjustment, while most inexpensive violins can be adjusted to sound acceptable.

The Adjustments

The violin must be tight, without open cracks and edges. A gentle knocking of the body and edges will reveal cracks and loose joints. Chinrest and tuners should be tight; chinrest and tailpiece must not touch the top of violin and/or each other.

The *bridge* must be well fitted by an expert and must have the proper curve and height. The strings must merely sit on notches half as deep as the string thickness. The notches should be protected against metal strings; a tiny piece of drumskin glued over the notches permanently protects the bridge and also gives the best tonal results. In localities where the seasonal changes in humidity are considerable, it is advisable to have two bridges, a lower one for humid weather. The bridge should be symmetrically set between the notches of the F hole (unless the measurement of the instrument is off, in which case the bridge can be placed differently to compensate), and it should often be pulled back with a firm grip over the top, to offset the tendency of the bridge to lean forward.

The *soundpost* should be fitted and placed by an expert. It should be set slightly behind the right leg of the bridge. A well-cut soundpost follows the contours of the top and back and must not be reversed or turned left or right when reset; a soundpost that is poorly set can scrape the inside of the top and seriously injure it.

The *fingerboard* should be smoothly planed, and without grooves at the string-contact line. It should be graduated to have a gently concave shape, with maximum depth at the string center. The nut at the end of the fingerboard must be evenly grooved. It should be exactly at a right angle to the fingerboard, and it must not be too high.

The *neck* should be well shaped. Avoid necks that have a narrow bottom; a mild, flat curve is advantageous. It should have a correct angle to the body, so that a normal bridge can bring the strings to proper elevation. The tension of the strings has a tendency to pull the neck forward from its original position; if the neck gives too much, it should be reset. The height of strings over the fingerboard depends on the angle of the neck and the height of the bridge and nut. Strings that are too high over the fingerboard cause left hand strain and make vibrato more difficult. The nut should be just high enough so that a visiting card (or paper, folded three times) slipped under the E string would be caught at the nut. The relative height of the strings, governed by the curve of the bridge, should be such that it provides enough clearance to permit playing *forte* on one string without hitting another.

Pegs, tuners. Pegs should turn smoothly without creaking, yet hold firmly. They should be adjusted from time to time and treated with "peg dope" (dry soap and chalk will do). For ease of tuning (the professional way), avoid setting the G and D pegs horizontally. *Tuners* are a must for metal strings. They should be set so as to allow sufficient tuning range in both directions.

Selection of strings. For best tonal results use steel E, aluminum-wound gut A and D, and silver-wound gut G strings. Do not combine metal core D and G strings with a gut core A string. Professionals match string gauges for evenness of response, using either thin, medium, or heavy gauges. Your string dealer can tell you about the correct matching of strings. If an instrument has a dull tone, it can be helped by the use of heavier strings, but this in turn will make it less responsive. Strings should be replaced when false or when wrapping gets loose. To check for false strings, tune them precisely, then press a cardboard piece across the string center at a right angle; check with the bow, and if the fifths are badly out of tune, replace the strings. Do not wait for the E string to break before replacement. E strings are notorious for getting false in short order, especially with sweaty fingertips. False strings make good intonation—especially in the higher positions—impossible.

Cleaning the instrument. This should be done regularly. Clean strings of rosin dust after each playing for better sound and maneuverability; more thoroughly, with a rag dipped in alcohol, twice a week or so. Do not touch varnish with alcohol. Clean the neck with a good violin cleaner every other day, and the whole instrument occasionally, to maintain its appearance.

Care of the bow. Always release the tension of the bow when through playing. The curve and the spring of the bow can be ruined with constant tension. If the loose bow is placed on a table, the lowest part of the stick should almost touch it; if not, the bow has lost its spring. Rosin the hair regularly, but sparingly. The bow should not "smoke" while drawing a strong tone. Use a good quality rosin; put fingers around the ferrule of the frog when applying rosin to prevent breaking it. The hair should be evenly set at the ferrule and tip. Uneven hair will warp the bow. Old, slick bow hair gets a thin, glossy sound. Re-hair bow after 300 hours of playing or sooner.

Suggested References

Flesch, Karl. *The Art of Violin Playing. Vol.1.* New York: Carl Fischer, Inc., 1924.
Hodgson, Percival. *Motion Study and Violin Bowing.* Urbana, Illinois: ASTA, 1958 (1934).
Seashore, Emil. *The Vibrato: University of Iowa Studies in the Psychology of Music.* Iowa City, Vol. I, 1932.
Steinhausen, F. A. *Die Physiologie der Bogenführung.* Leipzig: Breitkopf & Haertel, 1903.